How To Cook
ROADKILL

© Copyright 1986, 1988, 1991 Richard Marcou; 1993 MCB Publications
ISBN: 0-9637062-0-9

Cartoons, Cover, Text: Inspired by Richard Marcou
Cartoons, Cover: Illustrated by Randy Wall

Produced By: MCB Publications
              10922 Whisper Hollow, San Antonio, Texas 78230

Printed By: Publishers Press, USA

Preamble

All over North America, the world for that matter, hundreds of thousands of families are finding it ever more difficult to make ends meet; the highest single cost after the monthly commitment for a roof over one's head is the monthly food bill.

At the very same time our world over; hundreds of thousands of animals (birds, reptiles and insects) are killing themselves by coming into contact with moving vehicles on national highways, residential streets, country back roads and lanes. Approximately 193 million pounds of meat go unclaimed, not to mention the considerable amount of protein going to waste.

We would strongly suggest it's time hungry families and those wanting to increase their disposable incomes be shown how to benefit from the carnage on our highways. We feel the lack of available information on the subject has been the reason the two remain apart.

This void has now been finally filled with the exciting publication of **How To Cook Roadkill "Goremet Cooking".**

We also don't hesitate to point out further benefits such as:

— The growth of cottage industries - meat cutters, skin tanners, manufacturing of shoes, wallets, etc., a further reduction of the unemployed.

— The keeping of roadsides neat and tidy as well as reducing the bacteria count in the air.

— The filling of empty stomachs and freezers.

— Increasing the G.N.P.

— The formation of franchise opportunities like *The Roadkill Cafe.*

— The making of Sunday drives much less boring.

Drivers allowed to keep road kills

From the news services

NEWS ROUNDUP

TORONTO — A new regulation that allows motorists to take home any animals they accidentally kill on Ontario highways could lead to more poaching, says a spokesman for the Canadian Wildlife Federation.

The new legislation, effective today, could be abused by hunters shooting deer out of season, said Ken Brynaert.

Motorists first must notify the Natural Resources Ministry of the kill within 48 hours and receive written permission to take the animal. But not all reported road kills will be inspected by ministry officers.

========== **A Special Thanks** ==========

To my wife for her tolerance, support and understanding.

To the friends who thought this idea would fly and contributed their ideas and criticisms.

To Randy Wall, the talented artist.

To the guy by the roadside in northern Ontario cooking the rotten remnants of a raven; he sparked this whole idea.

Table of Contents

Stretching Your Food Dollars

Chapter One

Our mothers always told us *"waste not want not"*. We suggest that Roadkill is already dead, and in most cases you didn't do it; but that doesn't mean you can't benefit. Don't waste em! Eat em!

In a week, your average roadkill claims could easily be 10 pounds. Ten pounds of free meat per/week is about $1700 per/annum worth of stretching your food dollars.

Hey Folks! That is a holiday, new clothes, repairs to the beater you drive, or finally, cosmetic surgery to remove the warts with hair in them from your face.

Whatever you have thought to this point, forget it. The whole concept is to increase the amount of jingle in your purse or wallet.

We suggest you relax, loosen up a bit, smile; no one is watching. You may enjoy your warped sense of humour. It's bound to show through.

Give your cerebral cortex a shake and get on to the good stuff. Turn the page and become a waste-not-person, a connoisseur of *goremet* cooking.

Learning How To Identify Free Food; Quickly & Accurately At Sixty M.P.H.

Chapter Two

— Be alert to areas adjacent to fresh dark skid marks. Scan these areas quickly as in all probability you will be travelling at approximately 88 feet/second. A break in concentration could mean a missed opportunity.

— Always observe carefully areas with broken glass, headlight rims or body mouldings lying about. Check nearby trees in the event the animal became airborne with the force of impact.

— Close in on the area immediately below circling buzzards, crows and ravens, almost a certain sign of roadkill.

— A point to remember is that most of the time you should be looking for contrasts in colour.
  eg: Roadsides are usually green (grass), grey-brown (gravel), light brown (woods and dead grass).

Roadkill are usually lying on their backs exposing their white or light coloured bellies which is the contrast in colour you are looking for.

Prime Areas To Patrol

Chapter Three

Residential: Patrol the suburbs versus the core areas of a city because there is more affluence and more families have pets which in turn are better fed; as a result much more plump.
GOOD EATING!!

Highways: Due to the higher speeds on highways, animals have less chance of making it across. Keep an eye open for animal crossings, where animal traffic is usually heavy and presents a good opportunity of coming across roadkill.

Detours: Seek out detours because heavy traffic is new to animals and they are less wary; good chance of scoring on a recent hit.

Turkey Trucks: Follow These Trucks! They really pack em in. Every now and then one gets away and gets hit immediately.

Farmland: Farmers often drive herds across roads not to mention the strays you often see that have gotten through the fence. MOOOO!

Zoos: This is a great area, especially for birds like peacocks which often fly over the fences. (This area could be a real feather in your cap).

Schools: Often animals (pets) follow kids to school and are bewildered when the kids go inside. Good location for Kitty Creole or Bow Wow Chow fixings.

National Parks: Particularly good area as most animals are relatively tame and someone is bound to hit one the way they wander around the roads.

Prime Times To Patrol

Chapter Four

Winter vs. Summer: Year round patrolling in the northern parts of North America present benefits and disadvantages.

Patrolling in winter means old roadkill is well preserved because it freezes within a short time of being hit. Repeated snow falls quickly cover roadkill, making them difficult to spot. We suggest following high speed highway snow plows; keep alert for animals flying off the blade of the plow. Depending on the animal's size and the plow's speed, the roadkill could sail 20 feet off the roadside.
(Carry a pair of RKP snowshoes.)

Mealtimes: Most people feed their pets between 7 and 8 a.m. and between 4:30 and 6 p.m. then immediately let them out to relieve themselves. These times also happen to be heavy traffic hours so be alert to making the first claim.

Sunrise: Animal activity is high at this time. Patrol with the sun to your back so you can spot roadkill easily.

Night: Headlights blind animals and many meet their maker during this time. Ensure your vehicle has high powered lights to assist in spotting. Lights also reflect back at you from the eyes of live animals trying to steal your roadkill right out from under you. DON'T LET THEM DO IT!

Alterations & Equipment For Efficient Roadkill Patrol Vehicles

Chapter Five

Efficient Roadkill Patrol Vehicle

1) Roof mounted block & tackle
2) Winch
3) Headlight covers & brush guards
4) Heavy duty shocks
5) 12 volt 2 cu' fridge
6) Tailgate (for roadside meals)
7) Roof-mounted lights
8) Roof-mounted periscope
9) Radiation detector
10) First Aid Kit (bites & scratches)
11) Fire Extinguisher
12) Inflatable flotation device
13) Pots, pans, eating/cooking utensils.
14) Heavy duty cooking spices
15) Skin drying racks
16) Studded rear tires
17) Bug screen
18) Spare steel hubcap (Hub Cap-O-Soup)

Recipes

Chapter Six

While it hasn't been our intention to bring harm or discomfort to any individuals, we do feel inclined to advise that a certain degree of care be instituted if you plan to use any of these recipes. During the creation stages several people assisting in taste testing of our dishes developed severe gas to the point of grossly distended bellies accompanied by flatulence levels of over 93 decibals.

Within days most developed skin discoloration in conjunction with bad breath. In fact their breath was so bad that flies were falling off the walls in our testing facilities.

Some Points To Remember About Cooking Roadkill

— Most of these recipes can be prepared right at the location where roadkill is found. They can also be prepared at home using conventional appliances, barbecues and microwave ovens.

— Let all roadkill that is frozen thaw in a container of salt water, it acts as a tenderizer.

— Decomposition rates vary in North America. In Canada it's so cold that roadkill hit in September is good until April. In Florida, the maximum down time shouldn't exceed 72 hours.

— If you hit an animal by accident Remember: *You Hit It- You Eat It*.

Sideswipe Moose O' Shake & Bake

Ingredients: 1 600 lb. dead moose
35 lbs. of mixed spices to taste
6.2 litres of veggie oil

Preparation

1) Skin animal (save skin for wallets) and cut into eights.
2) Place pieces in a clean 45 gallon drum.
3) Add spices and oil.
4) Get 13 friends to help you shake the drum for 6 minutes to ensure meat is well coated.
5) Place drum on heat source for 22 minutes per 100 lbs.. It should be done standing well back; air pockets could explode showering you with hot fat.
6) Serves approximately 1,300 famished individuals.

Liver Splateé

Ingredients: 1 or more dead fox
2 tomatoes
1 onion
1/4 cup of veggie oil

Preparation

1) Skin fox using Quickie Skinning method (see Tips chapter). Save skin for mitts, tail for antenna of automobile.
2) Remove liver and place in skillet along with chopped tomatoes and onions.
3) Saute for 6 minutes until consistency of puree, drain fat and let cool.
4) Spread on bread. Serve with warm red wine.

* Hey Guys! This is a great sandwich for that foxy lady friend.

Bo-Peep Casserole "Lamb"

Ingredients: 1 small lamb
1 package of noodles
1 tin of stewed tomatoes
a handful of spices
a bucket of water from nearest ditch

Preparation

1) Skin lamb and eviscerate. (Utilize lamb skin for seat cover or dash of a Chevy van.)
2) Chop up lamb, place in cauldron. Add water and place on heat source. Bring water to boil for 1 hour.
3) Add tomatoes, noodles and spices. Boil a further 9 minutes.
4) Remove from heat and dig in - tastes Baaa! Iced tea goes well with this dish.

*Place sign beside road inviting other Roadkill Patrollers to join you.

Ewe will love it!

Bumper Bambee Fawn-Do

Ingredients: 1 small bambee
1 industrial size/strength package of cheese dip

Preparation

1) Skin bambee and place on fawn-do fork.
2) Cook over open fire, at the same time bring dip to a boil.
3) When bambee is done, remove from fire and place in dip for 10 minutes. Exquisite dish, tastes like chicken.
4) White wine is a must, preferably sweet.

*Discard skin, there isn't enough for anything but a small cushion cover.

Bow Wow Chow

Ingredients: 1 dead dawg
               1 bucket of assorted veggies
               1 cup of bay leaves, 1 cup of tarragon

Preparation

1) Place veggies in large cauldron with 4 litres of water. Boil for 20 minutes.
2) If dawg has hair, skin it. If not; just chop into bite size pieces.
3) While veggies are boiling, fry pieces of dawg in large skillet until brown. Add veggie oil if dawg was skinny.
4) When browned, drain, throw in with boiling veggies. Add spices and simmer another 25 minutes.

A *Doggone* Good Meal! Woof it down!

*Caution: After this meal resist the urge to chase cars.

Broken Back Bacon & Scrambled Legs

Ingredients: 1 pig with broken back
1 bucket of applesauce

Preparation

1) Eviscerate and clean the pig, remove 2 legs. Place the pig on a skewer then over fire. Pig's juices will self glaze, no need for barbecue sauce.
2) Break legs and place in skillet, stir fry over low heat until done.
3) Serves many people! Gives choice of barbecued or fried. A red bordeaux to wet your lips.

*If the pig is large and you don't wish to prepare it; then sell it at the nearest roadkill café. The owner has been trained to buy anything that comes along.

Lemming Meringue Pie "Dessert"

Ingredients: 8 lemmings per pie
1 packaged pie shell
1 cup of sugar
1 package of Meringue mix

Preparation

1) Gut and clean 8 lemmings; when dry, skin animals.
2) Place whole lemmings into pie crust and bake for 25 minutes at 325°.
3) While lemmings are baking, mix meringue and sugar.
4) Remove pie from oven, cover with meringue and bake further 6 minutes.
5) Slice and serve immediately with a glass of Muscatel or Tokay. Serves 8.

Turnpike Turnover "Dessert"

Ingredients: half dozen chipmunks
tube of pre-mixed puff pastry
1/4 cup of confectionary sugar
1/4 cup milk
6 acorns

Preparation

1) Skin and gut all chippies, wash thoroughly and place acorn in each mouth.
2) Divide tube of pastry into six portions; pat flat, and place chippie on one side of pastry.
3) Fold pastry over like taco and crimp shut. Brush with milk and sprinkle with sugar. Place on tray in oven at 375° for 40 minutes.

*Sew skins together. They make neat headbands.

Kitty Creole "Cajun Cooking"

Ingredients: 1 flat cat
               1 coffee can of carrots, peas and taters
               2 diced chile peppers and 1 bottle of hot sauce
               26 feet of foil

Preparation

1) Remove skin (very difficult when flat). If not flat enough when skinned, pass wheel over 1 more time.
2) Place cat on back, pile ALL ingredients onto belly and roll up like a cabbage roll.
3) Use 26 feet of foil and wrap thoroughly. Place on exhaust manifold. Cat will simmer in own juices & hot sauce as you drive. 150 miles should do it. If smoke appears you've driven too far.

Rearend Ragoût "Skunk"

Ingredients: 1 dead skunk
2 green peppers, 2 red peppers, 3 celery stalks
1/4 cup of veggie oil

Preparation

1) Place veggies and oil in large skillet and simmer.
2) Prepare skunk as depicted on left page.
3) Place gravy pan on heat source. When boiling, drain veggies from skillet and throw in pan. Add skunk chunks and let simmer for 2 hours. (While waiting wash your vehicle down.)
4) You could add a can of tomatoes to help reduce stench.

*Use strong nets as most chunks approach 100 M.P.H. from fan source. When finished eating, gargle with industro strength mouth wash.

Tongue In Cheek Pie With Udder Flambé

Ingredients: 1 cow's tongue and udder
1 pre-cooked pie shell and 1/4 lb. of ready dough
6 peeled potatoes
1 bottle of white wine

Preparation

Cow Pie: Cook and mash potatoes. Place potatoes in pie shell. Put tongue on top of potatoes. Let tongue hang out over edge and place dough over shell. Bake at 350° until tongue curls. Approximately 1 hour. (Serve with cold glass of milk.)

Flambé: If udder wasn't knocked off, cut it off. Scrape insides out and stretch over upside down bowl. Sprinkle with sugar and bake 30 minutes at 350°. Remove from oven and pour warm wine over udder, torch and serve.

*You may want to shave the hair off the tongue before cooking.
UDDERLY FANTASTIC!

===== **Legs Tornoff (Russian Dish)** =====

CO-CraBHaR: 1 OcuHɫ KoHb

            3 #Boe ra##oHɫ #eyeHie Mac#o

            2 Tp# ØyHrЪ ll3B MyKa

            2 #Boe #ЮXNHa RЙUo

NPuroToBreHie

1) OTAB#RTb Hora ec#N HTsTЪ y X e HCNO#HeHNbiЙ (KoXa #ĭ#aTb óo#bWoЙ HOCOKЪ)

2) OHTb RЙQO cb #OTb HavЪ Hora

3) #ØTb Myka BO OTPOXарeбyxa MĭWoKЪ cb TpRCTH BЪ KpBiTb 3CO Hora cb Myka.

4) Kan#R Hora BO ropHioKb cb r#yóokiЙ XapnTb N 30#otoЙ TeMHbiЙ.

* MyCTb ÓbiTb C#yXNTb cb HepHbiй pycKiй Nyet!!

18 Wheelers Delight — Hub Cap-O-Soup

Ingredients: 1 dead porcupine
             1 egg
             1 cup of noodles
             1 cup of Industro strength spices

Preparation

1) Cut fleshy part of belly out and dice. Discard the rest of the carcass.
2) Place 6 cups of water into hub cap and bring to a boil.
3) Add diced meat and all the remaining ingredients. Simmer for 30 minutes.

* After lunch pick your teeth with quill and be prepared for high levels of gas build-up.

Freeway Fricaseé "Turtle On The Cracked Shell"

Ingredients: 1 dead slowpoke
1 small bottle of dry white wine

Preparation

1) Place turtle upside down directly on heat source.
2) Pour wine down gullet. This will boil and enhance the meat flavor.
3) The turtle may hiss and shake as the steam escapes from the crack in the shell, no need for alarm, it won't explode.
4) When done (about 25 minutes) crack breast plate open with tire iron. Let cool and pick meat out with fingers.

*Any eggs found will be hard boiled, save for a snack.

Chile Con Carnage "Battered Bunny"

Ingredients: 1 battered bunny
2 tins of beans
2 chile peppers and 1/4 cup of vinegar

Preparation

1) Skin bunny (save feet for luck), chop into bits.
2) Place bunny bits, beans, peppers, vinegar and a cup of water in skillet.
3) Place on heat source, simmer 47 minutes whilst covered.

Great with a couple of cool ones or a bottle of full bodied dark red wine.

Froggy Croaketts

Ingredients: a whole mess of frogs
                1 package of stuffing mix
                several cups of bread crumbs

Preparation

1) Slit frogs from butt to chin and remove entrails, wash and pat dry.
2) Mix stuffing mix and bread crumbs with water; stuff frog cavities.
3) Place on platter under broiler for approximately 15 minutes. Remove when golden brown.
4) Immediately serve on bed of lily pads. Should be eaten like hors d'oeuvres.

A chablis is most appropriate.

Interstate Surprize "Creamed Chicken"

Ingredients: 1 chicken sans feathers
1 large can of mushrooms
1 cup of diced celery
1/4 cup of left over wine

Preparation

1) Most chickens loose feathers upon impact, if not AH! Pluck it.
2) Eviscerate, truss on skewer and roast over open flame until tender.
3) Whilst cooking chicken, saute in skillet remaining ingredients.
4) Break up chicken, place on platter and pour sauce over pieces.

Follow directions explicitly or this dish may leave a
fowl taste in your mouth.

Tips, Ethics & Unwritten Rules
Appendix, Cross Reference
Chapter Seven

— **Insects:** A last resort for some cultures, but it should be remembered that insects are high in protein and provide high roughage benefits. Depending on the area where you live, don't overlook the windshield, bumper, headlights and grill because a good days driving and 20 minutes of scraping should provide enough fixings to feed a family of three.

Great for a Quickie, Roadside, Easy, No Cooking
Splatter Platter

—Radioactivity: Because of the Chernobyl nuclear accident, check all roadkill with a geiger counter. Especially if its been lying around for a while.

—Quickie Skinning Tip: If alone, stake animal out near right rear wheel; if accompanied, have your partner hold on tight to the roadkill. Place foot on brake then slam the gas pedal down. This action should immediately remove the skin. This is called a break stand and it should be noted that you shouldn't try this with large animals like moose or cows with the transmission in reverse or you could wind up with the animal under your vehicle and the wheels off the ground.

—Meat Tenderizer: No need to overdue the exercise by tenderizing with a wooden mallet. Studded snow tires make a quick job of tenderizing meat; 2 or 3 passes back and forth should do it.

—Automated Dicer: Use with caution. Cover the distributor with a plastic bag, rev up the engine and toss dead animal into fan, works well! Great for dicing and defeathering birds, high revs will puree, always toss from left hand side as illustrated in Rearend Ragoût. Ensure fan blade has been sharpened.

—Gravel, Asphalt & Tar Remover: We are currently working in our labs attempting to produce a bio-degradable, non-toxic, non-allergenic gravel, tar and asphalt remover. Until then be careful, you could break or stain your teeth.

—Herbs and Spices: Use plenty of both as they tend to reduce cooking smells of some roadkill. They also considerably enhance the flavor. Use industrial strength only.

—Not Quite Dead Yet: Put the animal out of its misery by inducing a heart attack. Get your mother-in-law out of the vehicle and escort her back to the dying animal. The animal will GASP! (As you did the first time you saw her), lapse into shock which will prompt a cardiac arrest, death will be immediate (very humane and painless).

—Baiting: Never make a slow pass through a game preserve scattering cheap grain onto the road, waiting 10 minutes then turning around and driving back down the road at a high rate of speed (unethical).

—Second Hits: Never slam your vehicle into reverse and back up for a second hit on an injured animal. Not only is it unethical but its dangerous and could cause injury to yourself and occupants in oncoming traffic.

—First Claim To Roadkill: The first person to the animal always has first claim or rejection rights. In the event of a tie, the person with "*I Stop For Roadkill*" bumper sticker on their vehicle or the person wearing a Roadkill Patrol t-shirt has first rights (Remember the IRKS Creed about sharing).

Appendix
Mine were removed.

Cross Reference
Due to the nature of this book a cross reference isn't required.

Exciting "Roadkill Café" Franchise Opportunity
Chapter Eight

Advantages of a Roadkill Café Franchise

1) Head on management style utilized in selection of locations.
2) Unswerving loyalty to franchisee.
3) Group insurance rates through ET-YA Mutual.
4) Training in areas such as — Predicting consumer eating trends
   — On site eviscerations
   — Dead meat sales promotions
   — Hit of the Day menu selections
   — Curb your Kill programs
   — How to deal with people that don't like your business
   — Protection of territories

5) A very mobile business making access to meat supplies most desirable.
6) Consumers can buy a meal, or have their roadkill bulk wrapped to go at reasonable rates.
7) Curb your kill. Drop it off by 9 a.m.; ready by 5 p.m.. Packaged and wrapped to the consumer's wishes.
8) Mobility! Takes you to the people who buy. Sporting events, parades, fairs, protest marches, highway travellers, office and factory workers tired of brown bagging it and any gang fight you may come across.

=IRKS & Associated Roadkill= Personalizations
Chapter Nine

Great
Sound

Rock!!!

Blues!!

Country!!

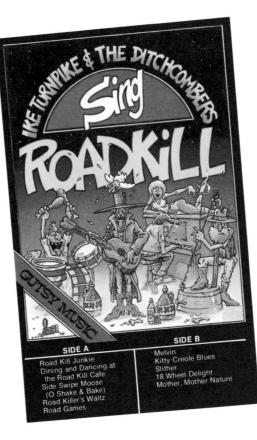

Sing along with
IKE,
SLY
BONE
KITTY
and
GIZZARD

Lyrics inside on J-card.

International Roadkill Specialists

As specialists we do it, not for the thrill
  But! We do live off the fixins of roadkill
  We treat them with dignity, so don't despair
We share with others, if there's a pair
  Bambee, Bow Wow, Bo-Peep and the rest
Once ran and frolicked along with the best
  We realize and keep foremost in our mind
  Some were peoples friends that we find.
We pledge to treat kindly others we meet
  On the highways to our freezers we'll be discreet
  At first it's difficult and some get ill
But soon its a challenge to patrol for roadkill.

Road hog

Woman dines on injured animals she finds along highway!

Most folks shop at the supermarket but Rachel Jackson hits the highway when she's looking for food. There she finds all the animals she needs to make dinners fit for a king!

"I've found dogs, cats and armadillos along the roadside while they were still wiggling," said the 56-year-old woman from Barberville, Fla.

Her wacky diet: Dogs, cats, snakes, possums and raccoons!

"In hopeless cases, I've put them out of their misery, brought them home, cooked them and eaten them. If they didn't taste good, I would feed them to the chickens."

More often than not, the road-kill critters she scrapes off the blacktop are delicious indeed. Sometimes she tops off a cat or dog dinner with a heaping helping of weeds!

"I believe that the world is headed for a famine and that food shouldn't be wasted," said Miss Jackson, who once taught college biology but is now unem-ployed and lives on a small pension.

"God put everything on this earth for us to use and appreciate, including plants and animals to eat.

"Rich people can buy what they want to eat," she continued. "Me, I don't have money. I pick up cats, dogs, raccoons, snakes and possums that have been hit by cars. If they're still warm, I catch them and eat them.

"If they're cold, I bury them."

Not surprisingly, Miss Jackson likes some animals better than others. Dogs, possums, raccoons, otters and armadillos have a strong, gamey flavor, she said.

Cats and snakes have a milder taste, she added, kind of like store-bought chicken!

Cooking road-kill critters is easier than one might think.

According to Miss Jackson, all you have to do is skin them and boil the meat "a real long time because they're tough." Then season to taste!

"You know, it would be real nice if everybody could be a vegetarian and even better if we could live on nothing but air," said Miss Jackson.

If She Can; You Can

By NAOMI LAKRITZ
Sun Staff Writer

Jill Oakes would rather pick up her groceries on the roadside than get them at Safeway.

The 33-year-old University of Manitoba student enjoys a varied menu that includes dead animals and songbirds squashed by passing cars, maggots, deer droppings, and the contents of elk and seal intestines.

"Why would I want to eat storebought food? I have different standards of when food is rotten — because I eat rotten food," said Oakes, a post-graduate student specializing in Inuit textiles.

As a child on Vancouver Island, Oakes enjoyed wild venison, duck and even earthworms, but she acquired her more exotic culinary tastes after visiting the Baffin Island Inuit.

"I ate what they ate and enjoyed it. That included seal brains, seal eyeballs, raw lungs and liver and the contents of the animals' intestines and stomachs. I have eaten stuff that would make a parasitologist freak out, like Bott's fly larvae that grow in the throats of caribou," she said.

Back home in Winnipeg, Oakes cruises country roads for her next meal of rabbit, porcupine or birds. She said she once picked up a dead cat but it was too far gone for consumption.

"Domestic animals could be dangerous to eat because you don't know what they've been into. I wouldn't eat the droppings from dogs or coyotes but I would eat them raw from a caribou or deer. They contain protein," she said.

Oakes doesn't care how she finds her food — mangled by other animals, shot by hunters or flattened by cars. She'll also cook up the maggots that infest the corpses because they're "pure protein — nothing wrong with that."

Songbirds often have an unpleasant taste, but Oakes scoops them up anyway because she says she's competing for that food with animals who might otherwise take it.

"When all this stuff is cooked up, it could be chicken, beef or pork except for the taste. I boil it, bake it or put it in the wok," Oakes said.

She began exploring yet another dimension of exotic eating when she moved into a maggot and moth-infested house last fall.

"I was sitting down for supper and a moth fell in my plate so I ate it. Then I looked around for others. There were crocks of flour filled with maggots so I made the stuff into bread."

She said the bread rose beautifully because the maggots hatched with the heat of the baking, beat their wings and helped round out the loaf.

Reprinted with permission of the Winnipeg Sun.

If you are unable to obtain additional copies of this book from your local book store, then send check or money order to:

MCB Publications
10922 Whisper Hollow, San Antonio, Texas 78230
1-210-492-2358
$9.95 (plus $3.50 postage and handling)
Texas residents add 8 $\frac{1}{4}$% for tax